HOOKED SCARVES

HOOKED SCARVES

20 Easy Crochet Projects

MARGARET HUBERT

Creative Publishing
international

CHANHASSEN, MN

For my wonderful grandchildren, the sunshine of my life.

Acknowledgments

I wish to thank Alchemy Yarns, Berroco Inc., Blue Heron Yarns, Caron Yarn Co., Lion Brand Yarn Co., Patons Yarns, Plymouth Yarns, Tahki/Stacy Charles Yarns, and Trendsetter Yarns who so graciously supplied yarns for most of the projects in this book. Thanks to Jeannine Buehler, Paula Alexander, and Grace Gardiner for helping me crochet some of the projects in the book. Thank you to Linda Neubauer, my editor, always a joy to work with.

Creative Publishing
international

Copyright 2007
Creative Publishing international
18705 Lake Drive East
Chanhassen, Minnesota 55317
1-800-328-3895
www.creativepub.com
All rights reserved

President/CEO: Ken Fund

Executive Editor: Alison Brown Cerier

Executive Managing Editor: Barbara Harold

Senior Editor: Linda Neubauer

Photo Stylist: Joanne Wawra

Creative Director: Brad Springer

Photo Art Director: Tim Himsel

Photographer: Steve Galvin

Production Manager: Laura Hokkanen

Cover and Book Design: Dania Davey

Page Layout: Lois Stanfield

Printed in China

10 9 8 7 6 5 4 3 2

Hubert, Margaret.
  Hooked scarves : 20 easy crochet projects / Margaret Hubert.
    p. cm.
  ISBN-13: 978-1-58923-268-6 (soft cover)
  ISBN-10: 1-58923-268-2 (soft cover)
  1. Crocheting--Patterns. 2. Scarves. I. Title.
  TT825.H79857 2006
  746.43'40432--dc22   2006012594

All the yarns used in this book can be found or ordered at your local yarn shop or craft store. Visit the following web sites for more information about the yarns shown:

Alchemy Yarns of Transformation
www.alchemyyarns.com

Berroco, Inc.
www.berroco.com

Blue Heron Yarns
www.blueheronyarn.com

Brown Sheep Company, Inc.
www.brownsheep.com

Caron International
www.caron.com

Katia Yarns/Knitting Fever
www.knittingfever.com

Lion Brand Yarn Company
www.lionbrand.com

On Line Yarns/Knitting Fever
www.knittingfever.com

Patons Yarns
www.patonsyarns.com

Plymouth Yarn Company
www.plymouthyarn.com

Sirdar Spinning Company
www.sirdar.co.uk

Tahki/Stacy Charles, Inc.
www.tahkistacycharles.com

Wool Pak Yarns NZ
www.baabajoeswool.com

Contents

About the Projects

Scarves are the most popular crochet project of all. No wonder, as crocheted scarves are fun, fast, and in fashion. Most beginners make a scarf first, and crocheters keep right on making them, especially when they want to indulge in special yarns. After all, is it possible to have too many scarves?

With this collection of my original patterns, you can make a whole scarf wardrobe. The projects include both fashion scarves for day or evening, and cozy scarves to keep you warm. A crocheted scarf can be as light as lace, or as thick as a muffler—it all depends on the yarns and the stitches. A scarf is a great gift, too, so included are styles to suit everyone on your list.

I have used stitches from simple single crochet to more intricate basket weave, lace, and bobbles. Some of the scarves are especially easy and are good beginner projects. Some projects are a bit more challenging, but they offer good chances to learn new stitches. If you need to learn or review a stitch, just go to "Crochet Stitches" that begins on page 80, which has detailed, photographed instructions.

For each project, I chose a yarn to complement the stitch and the design of the scarf. Smooth yarns show off the texture of crochet and are good for decorative stitches like shells, bobbles, basket weaves, or lace—and they make even single crochet look fascinating. Some scarves are made with bulky-weight yarns and crocheted with large hooks, and they work up really fast. Novelty yarns give other scarves special character, from furry and fun to glitzy and dramatic.

I have used a wide variety of yarns, including the great basics you can buy at fabric, craft, and department stores, and the designer and specialty products at yarn shops. The materials lists tell you the weight and type of each yarn, as well as the brands and colors I used. You can copy mine exactly, choose your own colors, or substitute different yarns of the same weight.

Don't be afraid to experiment with the inspiring yarns in the stores today. A scarf won't take all that much yarn! Because scarves don't have to fit, gauge is not too important. If your scarf turns out a little wider or longer, it won't affect the wear. If your work is too tight, though, you may want to use a larger hook, so that your scarf will be soft.

Grab your hook and yarn, relax, and have fun!

Margaret Hubert is also the author of Hooked Bags, Hooked Hats, Hooked Throws, How to Free-Form Crochet, *and six other books. She designs crochet projects for yarn companies and magazines and teaches at yarn shops, retreats, and national gatherings.*

Surprise Me Striped Scarf

This fun yarn is dyed in such a way that a vibrant striped pattern forms naturally as you work. Add an easy textured stitch, and you've got a fabulous look in no time at all.

YARN

Medium-weight variegated wool yarn

Shown: Kureyon by Noro, 100% wool, 1.75 oz (50 g)/110 yd (100 m): #130, 3 skeins

HOOK

Size 10½/K (6.5 mm)

STITCHES USED

Single crochet

Double crochet

GAUGE

4 clusters = 4" (10 cm) on 10½/K hook

NOTIONS

Tapestry needle

8" (20 cm) piece of cardboard

FINISHED SIZE

6" (15 cm) wide and 48" (122 cm) long

Self-striping wool yarn changes colors as you crochet.

SCARF

Foundation row: Ch 21. Starting in third ch from hook, work 2 dc in ch, * sk 2 ch, [1 sc, 2 dc] in next ch, rep from * to last 3 ch, sk 2 ch, 1 sc in last ch, ch 1 (counts as sc), turn.

Row 1: Work 2 dc in first st, * sk 2 dc, [1 sc, 2 dc] in next sc, rep from * to last 3 sts, sk 2 dc, 1 sc in top of the tch, turn.

Rep row 1 for 48" (122 cm) from beg.

FINISHING

1. Weave in ends using tapestry needle.
2. To create fringe, wind yarn several times around an 8" (20 cm) piece of cardboard, cut one end. Rep until 90 16" (40 cm) strands have been cut. Holding 3 strands together for each fringe, fold strands in half, insert a crochet hook from back to front through the right-hand corner of one scarf end, and pull the folded end of the strands through the scarf. Bring strand ends through the loop and pull firmly to knot. Rep across for a total of 15 knots on each end of scarf. Trim fringe even if necessary.

Scarf ends are finished with luxuriously long fringe.

Dainty Shells Scarf

Feminine in a plush chenille yarn, this scarf showcases the pretty shell stitch. Front post and back post double crochet adds a subtle depth and definition to the overall pattern, and the shell stitch appears again in the edging.

YARN

Medium-weight cotton/rayon chenille yarn

Shown: Velourine by Fonty, 54% cotton/46% viscose, 1.75 oz (50 g)/120 yd (110 m): #608, 3 skeins

HOOK

Size 8/H (5 mm)

STITCHES USED

Double crochet

Front post double crochet

Back post double crochet

GAUGE

$3\frac{1}{2}$ shell clusters = 4" (10 cm) on 8/H hook

NOTION

Tapestry needle

FINISHED SIZE

5" (13 cm) wide and 60" (152 cm) long

Front post and back post double crochet stitches form ridges between shells.

SCARF

First half of scarf is worked first, then second half is picked up from beg of first half and worked out to the end.

Foundation row: Ch 26. Starting in fifth ch from hook, work [2 dc, ch 1, 2 dc] in same ch (shell cluster), * sk 2 ch, work 1 dc in next ch, sk 2 ch, work [2 dc, ch 1, 2 dc] in next ch. Rep from * across, 1 dc in last ch, ch 3, turn.

Row 1: * Work [2 dc, ch 1, 2 dc] in ch-1 sp, FPdc in dc, rep from * across, [2 dc, ch 1, 2 dc] in ch-1 sp, dc in top of tch, ch 3, turn.

Row 2: * Work [2 dc, ch 1, 2 dc] in ch-1 sp, BPdc in dc, rep from * across, [2 dc, ch 1, 2 dc] in ch-1 sp, dc in top of tch, ch 3, turn.

Rep rows 1 and 2 for 28" (71 cm) from beg, end row 2. Work edging as foll:

Both ends of the scarf are finished with scalloped edging.

EDGING

Row 1: * Work [3 dc, ch 2, 3 dc] in ch-1 sp, FPdc in dc, rep from * across, [3 dc, ch 2, 3 dc] in ch-1 sp, dc in top of tch, ch 3, turn.

Row 2: * Work [4 dc, ch 2, 4 dc] in ch-2 sp, BPdc in dc, rep from * across, [4 dc, ch 2, 4 dc] in ch-2 sp, dc in top of tch, ch 3, turn.

Row 3: * Work [4 dc, ch 2, 4 dc] in ch-2 sp, FPdc in dc, rep from * across, [4 dc, ch 2, 4 dc] in ch-2 sp, dc in top of tch, ch 3, turn. Fasten off.

SECOND HALF OF SCARF

Join yarn in right corner of beg of scarf, ch 3.

Foundation row: Work [2 dc, ch 1, 2 dc] in same ch as cluster, * sk 2 ch, work 1 dc in same ch as dc, sk 2 ch, work [2 dc, ch 1, 2 dc] in same ch as cluster. Rep from * across, 1 dc in same ch as last dc, ch 3, turn.

Cont with row 1 of scarf, rep scarf and edging as for first half. Fasten off.

FINISHING

Weave in ends using tapestry needle.

Raspberry Puff Scarf

A soft, lacy, puff-stitch pattern in a beautifully

draping ribbon yarn creates a scarf for any

season. Make it bright and bold, or in a soft

shade for a vintage look. A trellis shell stitch

pattern finishes the ends.

YARN

Medium-weight rayon ribbon

Shown: Glacé by Berroco, 100% rayon, 1.75 oz (50 g)/75 yd (69 m): Shock #2518, 3 skeins

HOOK

Size 8/H (5 mm)

STITCHES USED

Single crochet

Double crochet

Puff stitch

GAUGE

3 puff sts = 4" (10 cm) on 8/H hook

NOTION

Tapestry needle

FINISHED SIZE

5" (13 cm) wide and 46" (117 cm) long

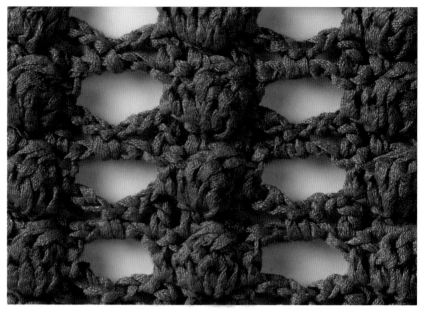

Rayon ribbon yarn is hooked in double-crochet clusters called puff stitches.

SCARF
Scarf is worked lengthwise.

Foundation row: Ch 129. Starting in fourth ch from hook, work 1 dc, * ch 2, sk next ch, 1 sc in next ch, ch 2, sk next ch, 1 dc in each of next 3 ch, rep from * across, 1 dc in each of last 2 ch, ch 3 (counts as dc now and throughout), turn.

Row 1: Sk first st, 1 dc in next st, * ch 3, 1 dc in first dc of 3-dc cluster, 1 puff st in next dc, 1 dc in next dc, rep from * across, ch 3, 1 dc in next dc, 1 dc in top of tch, ch 3, turn.

Row 2: Sk first st, 1 dc in next st, * ch 2, 1 sc in ch-3 sp, ch 2, 1 dc in next dc, 1 dc in puff st, 1 dc in next dc, rep from * across, ch 2, 1 sc in ch-3 sp, ch 2, 1 dc in next dc, 1 dc in top of tch, ch 3, turn.

Rep rows 1 and 2 four times more (5 puff st rows in all), end row 2, do not fasten off. Ch 1, turn to work along end of scarf, work edging as foll:

EDGING
Foundation row: Work 25 sc across end of scarf, ch 3, turn.

Row 1: Work 2 dc in first st, sk 2 sts, 1 sc in next st, ch 6, sk 5 sts, 1 sc in next st, sk 2 sts, 5 dc in next sc (shell made), sk 2 sts, 1 sc in next sc, ch 6, sk 5 sts, 1 sc in next st, ch 2, sk 2 sts, 3 dc in last st, ch 1, turn.

Main scarf is worked side to side. Several rows of lacy openwork are added at each end.

Row 2: Work 1 sc in first st, ch 5, 1 sc in ch-5 sp, ch 5, 1 sc in third dc of shell, ch 5, 1 sc in ch-5 sp, ch 5, 1 sc in top of tch, ch 5, turn.

Row 3: Work *1 sc in ch-5 sp, 5 dc in next st, 1 sc in ch-5 sp, ch 5, 1 sc in ch-5 sp, 5 dc in next st, 1 sc in ch-5 sp, ch 2, 1 dc in top of tch, ch 1, turn.

Row 4: Work 1 sc in first st, ch 5, 1 sc in third dc of shell, ch 5, 1 sc in ch-5 sp, ch 5, 1 sc in third dc of shell, ch 5, 1 sc in third ch of tch, ch 3, turn.

Row 5: Work 2 dc in first st, 1 sc in ch-5 sp, ch 5, 1 sc in ch-5 sp, 5 dc in next st, 1 sc in ch-5 sp, ch 5, 1 sc in ch-5 sp, 3 dc in top of tch, ch 1, turn.

Rep rows 2–5 once more, then rep rows 2–3, fasten off.

Work other end of scarf to correspond.

FINISHING
Weave in ends using tapestry needle.

The Dazzler

A cross-hatch stitch shows off the wonderful colors

in this hand-dyed yarn. The unusual pattern, the

elegant drape, and a touch of glitz make this scarf

right for a night out.

YARN

Lightweight rayon/metallic yarn

Shown: Rayon Metallic by Blue Heron Yarns, 85% rayon/15% metallic, 8 oz (227 g)/550 yd (506 m): Sunset, 1 skein

HOOK

Size 6/G (4.5 mm)

STITCHES USED

Single crochet

Double crochet

GAUGE

4 clusters = 4" (10 cm) on 6/G hook

NOTION

Tapestry needle

FINISHED SIZE

6" (15 cm) wide and 50" (127 cm) long

Lightweight, multicolored, rayon/metallic yarn worked in double crochet clusters.

SCARF

Foundation row: Ch 50. Starting in fourth ch from hook, work 2 dc in ch, sk 3 ch, 1 sc in next ch, * ch 3, dc in each of next 3 ch, sk 3 ch, sc in next ch, rep from * across, ch 3, turn.

Row 1: Work 2 dc in first st * sk next 3 dc [1 sc, ch 3, 3 dc] in next ch-3 sp, sk next st, rep from * across, sk last 2 sts, sc in top of tch.

Rep row 1 for 50" (127 cm) from beg.

FINISHING

1. To create a tassel, cut two 18" (46 cm) pieces of yarn and set aside to use for ties. Cut eight 12" (30.5 cm) pieces of yarn; using one of the 18" pieces, tie the 12" pieces together in center and fold in half. Leave the 18" piece to tie tassel to scarf. Wrap the second 18" piece around tassel about $\frac{1}{2}$" (1.25 cm) down from top. Do not cut; the ends will become part of tassel. Rep until 14 tassels are completed (7 for each end of scarf). Using tapestry needle and yarn tied at center of tassel, attach one tassel to each ch-3 sp at end of scarf.
2. Weave in ends using tapestry needle.

Slim tassels hang from three-chain spaces at the ends of the scarf.

Big Puffs Scarf

The contrasting textures of two yarns blend
beautifully in this eye-catching scarf. Made with a
very large hook and big, puffy stitches, this scarf
can be whipped up in an evening.

YARN

Medium-weight wool/mohair
blend yarn

Shown: Wonderful Wool
by Steadfast Fibers,
85% wool/15% mohair,
4 oz (113 g)/190 yd (175 m):
Groovy Green, 1 skein (A)

Bulky-weight mohair yarn

Shown: Marvelous Mohair by
Steadfast Fibers, 74%
mohair/13% wool/13% nylon,
2 oz (57 g)/110 yd (101 m):
Groovy Green, 1 skein (B)

HOOK

Size 11/L (8 mm)

STITCHES USED

Single crochet

Double crochet

Loose puff stitch

GAUGE

1 loose puff st = 1" (2.5 cm)
on 11/L hook

NOTIONS

Tapestry needle

8" (20 cm) piece of cardboard

FINISHED SIZE

4" (10 cm) wide and 60"
(152 cm) long

Rows of mohair yarn alternate with rows of smooth wool/mohair yarn in loose puff stitches.

SCARF

When changing yarns, do not fasten off. Instead, carry yarn loosely up sides.

Foundation row: With A, ch 20. Starting in 5th ch from hook, yo, pick up a long loop [at least ½" (1.3 cm)], yo, pull through 2 loops * yo, pick up a loop in next ch, yo, pull through 2 loops *, rep from * to * 3 times, yo, pull through all 6 loops (first foundation puff made), ch 1, rep from * to * 5 times, (second foundation puff made), ch 1, rep from * to * 5 times, (3rd foundation puff made), 1 dc in last ch, ch 3, turn.

Row 1: Work 1 loose puff st in first ch-1 sp, ch 1, * loose puff st in next ch-1 sp, ch 1, rep from * once, 1 dc in top of tch, pull up B in last lp, ch 3 with B, turn.

Row 2: With B, rep row 1.

Row 3: Rep row 1. Pull up A in last lp, ch 3 with A, turn.

Row 4: With A, rep row 1.

Rep rows 1–4 for 60" (152 cm), end row 1. Fasten off both yarns.

Entire scarf is edged with single crochet. Ends are finished with fringe using only the smooth yarn.

EDGING

Join B in bottom right-hand corner of scarf, * work 1 row sc along long side of scarf, working 3 sc in each sp formed by tchs and 2 sc in each side of loose puff st. Work 3 sc in last st to form corner, 10 sc along short end of scarf, 3 sc in last st to form corner. Rep from *, Sl st in first sc, fasten off.

FINISHING

1. Weave in ends using tapestry needle.

2. To create fringe, wind yarn several times around an 8" (20 cm) piece of cardboard, cut one end. Rep until 60 16" (40 cm) strands have been cut. Holding 3 strands together for each fringe, fold strands in half, insert a crochet hook from back to front through the right-hand corner of one scarf end, and pull the folded end of the strands through the scarf. Bring strand ends through the loop and pull firmly to knot. Rep across for a total of 10 knots on each end of scarf. Trim fringe even if necessary.

Scattered Flowers Ascot

This hip scarf is crocheted in an open stitch that

allows the mohair fibers in the yarn to bloom. Lots of

fluffy flowers and a fresh color make it fun to wear;

the quick, easy mesh pattern makes it fun to crochet.

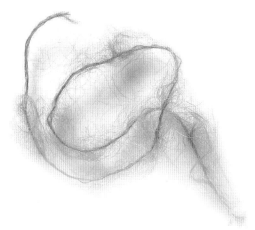

YARN
Medium-weight mohair yarn

Shown: Ingenua by Katia, 78% mohair/13% nylon/9% wool, 1.75 oz (50 g)/153 yd (141 m): Orange #17, 1 skein

HOOK
Size 6/G (4.5 mm)

STITCHES USED
Single crochet

Double crochet

GAUGE
7 mesh sts = 4" (10 cm) on 6/G hook

NOTION
Tapestry needle

FINISHED SIZE
5" (13 cm) wide and 36" (91.5 cm) long

29

Mohair yarn hooked in an open lattice pattern forms the scarf foundation.

SCARF

Foundation row: Ch 20. Starting in sixth ch from hook, work 1 dc, *ch 1, sk 1 ch, 1 dc in next ch, rep from * across (9 dc, 8 ch-1 sps), ch 4 (counts as dc, ch 1), turn.

Row 1: Work 1 dc in next st, * ch 1, 1 dc in next st, rep from * across, work last dc in third ch of beg ch 4.

Rep row 1 for 36" (91.5 cm), fasten off. Make flowers as foll:

FLOWERS

Make 19, set aside.

Foundation rnd: Ch 4, join with Sl st to form ring, work 10 sc in ring, join with a Sl st.

Rnd 1: * Ch 2, 3 dc in next st, ch 2, Sl st in next st, rep from * 4 times more (5 petals), fasten off.

FINISHING

1. Using the loose ends from begs of flowers, sew flowers onto ascot, scattering them randomly. Sew down centers only, leaving petals free.
2. Weave in ends using tapestry needle.

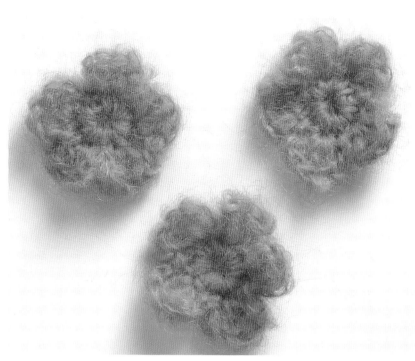

Simple five-petal flowers are crocheted separately and sewn to the scarf.

Little Hands Warmer

This scarf is as practical as it is fun; there are

pockets at each end for warming up those cute

little hands. Children will love the bright colors,

and the solid stitch pattern will keep them warm.

Add colorful flowers for a girl,

omit them for a boy's scarf.

YARN

Medium-weight acrylic/wool yarn in four colors

Shown: Encore by Plymouth Yarn Company, 75% acrylic/25% wool, 3.5 oz (100 g)/200 yd (184 m): #1383, 1 skein (A); #4045, 1 skein (B); #3335, 1 skein (C); #1386, 1 skein (D)

HOOK

Size 10/J (6 mm)

STITCHES USED

Single crochet

Half double crochet

Double crochet

GAUGE

6 small shells = 4" (10 cm) on 10/J hook

NOTION

Tapestry needle

FINISHED SIZE

5" (13 cm) wide and 37" (94 cm) long

Acrylic/wool yarn hooked in a mini-shell pattern creates a soft, warm fabric.

SCARF

Scarf is made in 2 pieces and joined at center. Pockets and flowers are made separately and sewn on.

Foundation row: With A, ch 22. Starting in third ch from hook, * work [1 sc, ch 2, 1 sc] in next ch, sk 2, rep from *, 1 hdc in last ch, (7 small shells), ch 2 (counts as hdc now and throughout), turn.

Row 1: * Work [1 sc, ch 2, 1 sc] in ch-2 sp of small shell, rep from * across, 1 hdc in top of tch.

Rep row 1 for 26 rows. Fasten off A, join B.

Rep row 1 for 26 rows. Fasten off B, join C.

Rep row 1 for 26 rows. Fasten off C, join D.

Rep row 1 for 14 rows, fasten off.

Rep from beginning for second half of scarf.

POCKETS

Make 2.

With A, ch 22. Work same as first 26 rows of scarf. Fasten off.

Crocheted posies accent the pockets at the scarf ends.

FLOWERS
Make 2 each in B, C, and D.

Foundation rnd: Ch 4, join with Sl st to form a ring, work 10 sc in ring, join with Sl st in first sc.

Rnd 1: * Ch 2, 3 dc in next st, ch 2, Sl st in next st, rep from * 4 times more (5 petals), fasten off.

FINISHING
1. Using a tapestry needle and the loose ends from scarf ends, sew scarf pieces together at center (D forms a full color block).
2. Using the loose ends from begs of flowers, sew flowers onto pockets, if desired, sewing down centers only and leaving petals free.
3. Using a strand of A, sew pockets to scarf ends, covering A blocks.
4. Weave in ends using tapestry needle.

Picot Mesh Scarf

Pamper yourself with a silk-blend scarf in an elegant and easy

picot mesh stitch. The scarf is soft,

luxurious, and sophisticated. For a crisper,

more casual look, try this scarf in a

shiny cotton/rayon blend.

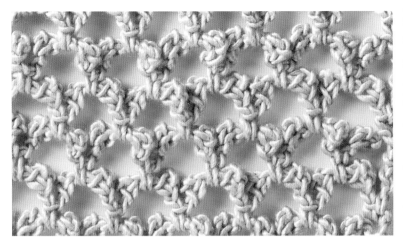
Luxurious silk/wool blend yarn hooked in a dainty picot mesh pattern.

SCARF

Foundation row: Ch 30. Work 1 sc in second ch from hook* [ch 4, 1 sc in third ch from hook (picot made)] twice, ch 1, sk 4 chs, 1 sc in next ch, rep from * across (6 ch-4 sps), ch 9 (counts as 1 dc, ch 4), turn.

Row 1: Work 1 sc in third ch from hook, ch 1, 1 sc in center of 2 picots, * [ch 4, 1 sc in 3rd ch from hook] twice, ch 1, 1 sc between 2 picots, rep from * across, ch 4, 1 sc in 3rd ch from hook, 1 dtr in last sc, ch 1, turn.

Row 2: Work 1 sc in first dtr, * [ch 4, 1 sc in third ch from hook] twice, ch 1, 1 sc between 2 picots, rep from * across, 1 sc in fifth ch of beg ch 9.

Rep rows 1 and 2 for 50" (127 cm) end row 2, fasten off.

Join yarn in the right-hand corner of other end of scarf, ch 9, work rows 1 and 2 once only, as foll:

Row 1: Work 1 sc in third ch from hook, ch 1, 1 sc in next sp, * [ch 4, 1 sc in third ch from hook] twice, ch 1, 1 sc in next sp, rep from * across, ch 4, 1 sc in third ch from hook, ch 1, 1 dtr in last st, ch 1, turn.

Row 2: Work 1 sc in first dtr, * [ch 4, 1 sc in third ch from hook] twice, ch 1, 1 sc between 2 picots, rep from * across, 1 sc in the fifth ch of beg ch 9. Fasten off.

FINISHING

Weave in ends using tapestry needle.

YARN
Medium-weight silk/wool blend yarn

Shown: Synchronicity by Alchemy Yarns, 50% silk/50% merino wool, 1.75 oz (50 g)/110 yd (101 m): 47w Pale Blue Eyes, 2 skeins

HOOK
Size 8/H (5 mm)

STITCHES USED
Single crochet

Double triple crochet

GAUGE
3½ clusters = 4" (10 cm) on 8/H hook

NOTION
Tapestry needle

FINISHED SIZE
5" (13 cm) wide and 50" (127 cm) long

Garden Trellis Scarf

The unusual stitch in this scarf looks like a trellis

of flowers. The effect is achieved by combining

clusters of triple crochet with openwork.

YARN

Medium-weight cotton/rayon blend bouclé yarn

Shown: Handpainted Yarn by Spectrum Yarns, cotton/rayon blend, 8 oz (225 g)/585 yd (538 m): Komoto Dragon, 1 skein

HOOK

Size 8/H (5 mm)

STITCHES USED

Single crochet

Double crochet

Triple crochet

Triple crochet 2 together

Double triple crochet

GAUGE

2 clusters = 4" (10 cm) on 8/H hook

NOTION

Tapestry needle

FINISHED SIZE

6" (15 cm) wide and 64" (162 cm) long

Cotton/rayon bouclé yarn crocheted in alternating rows of flowers and lattice.

SCARF

Foundation row: Ch 35. Starting in eighth ch from hook, work 1 dc, * ch 2, sk 2 ch, 1 dc into next ch, rep from * (10 ch-2 sps), ch 1, turn.

Row 1: Work 1 sc in first dc, * ch 9, sk 1 dc, [1 sc, ch 4, 1 tr2tog] in next dc, sk 1 dc, [1 tr2tog, ch 4, 1 sc] in next dc, rep from * once, ch 9, sk 1 dc, 1 sc in third ch of tch (3 ch-9 loops, 2 clusters), ch 10 (counts as dtr, ch 4), turn.

Row 2: Work 1 sc in first ch-9 sp, * ch 4, [1 tr2tog, ch 4, 1 Sl st, ch 4, 1 tr2tog] in top of next tr2tog, ch 4, 1 sc in next ch-9 sp, rep from * once, ch 4, 1 dtr in last sc, (6 ch-4 lps, 2 clusters), ch 1, turn.

Row 3: Work 1 sc in first dtr, * ch 5, 1 sc in top of next tr2tog, rep from * across, ch 5, 1 sc in sixth ch of tch, (5 ch-5 sp), ch 5, (counts as 1 dc, ch 2), turn.

Row 4: Work 1 dc in next ch-5 sp, ch 2, 1 dc in next sc, *ch 2, 1 dc in next ch-5 sp, ch 2, 1 dc in next sc, rep from * across (10 ch-2 sps), ch 1, turn.

Rep rows 1–4 for 62" from beg, end row 4. Work edging as foll:

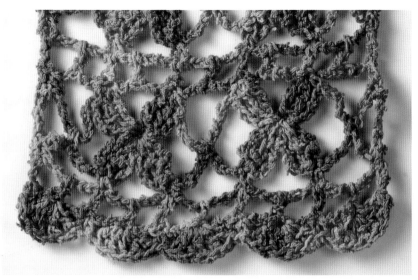
Shell edging finishes the scarf ends.

EDGING

Row 1: Sk first dc, work 5 dc in next dc, 1 sc in next dc, * 5 dc in next dc, 1 sc in next dc, rep from * across (5 shells), fasten off.

Join yarn in right-hand corner at other end of scarf, ch 1, rep row 1 of edging.

FINISHING

Weave in ends using tapestry needle.

Clever Blocks Scarf

An interlocking block stitch is fun to do and produces

intriguing results, especially when a glitzy yarn is

mixed with a soft, natural-looking yarn. Like the stitch

pattern itself, the scarf is a little offbeat—perfect with

a denim jacket as well as a tailored coat.

YARN

Medium-weight alpaca/wool yarn in two colors

Shown: Suri Merino by Plymouth Yarn Company, 55% Suri alpaca/45% extra-fine merino wool, 1.75 oz (50 g)/109 yd (100 m): #282, 1 ball (A); #208, 1 ball (C)

Medium-weight metallic ladder yarn

Shown: Eros Glitz by Plymouth Yarn Company, 86% nylon/10% rayon/4% Lurex, 1.75 oz (50 g)/158 yd (145 m): #117, 1 ball (B)

HOOK

Size 9/I (5.5 mm)

STITCHES USED

Single crochet

Double crochet

Interlocking block stitch

GAUGE

17 dc = 4" (10 cm) on 9/I hook

NOTIONS

Tapestry needle

8" (20 cm) piece of cardboard

FINISHED SIZE

5" (13 cm) wide and 54" (137 cm) long

Metallic ladder yarn interlocks with smooth alpaca/wool yarn for unexpected texture variations.

SCARF

Work one row each in colors A, B, and C throughout, carrying yarn loosely up sides.

Foundation row: With A, ch 23. Starting in fourth ch from hook, work 1 dc into each of next 2 ch, * ch 3, sk 3 ch, 1 dc into each of the next 3 ch, rep from * twice more (4 groups of 3 dc, 3 sps), pull up B in last lp, ch 3 with B, turn.

Row 1: With B, * sk next 3 sts, 1 dc in each of next 3 ch that were skipped in foundation ch (working over and enclosing ch-3 created in foundation row), ch 3, rep from * 2 times more, sc in top of tch, pull up C in last lp, ch 3 with C (counts as dc), turn.

Row 2: With C, sk first st, 1 dc in each of next 2 sts that were skipped in row below (working over and enclosing ch-3 created in previous row) * ch 3, sk 3 sts, 1 dc in each of next 3 sts that were skipped in row below, rep from * twice, pull up A in last lp, ch 3 with A, turn.

Row 3: With A, *sk next 3 sts, 1 dc in each of the next 3 sts that were

Fringe is made from strands of all three yarns.

skipped in row below (working over and enclosing ch-3 created in previous row), rep from * 2 times more, ch 3, sc in top of the turning ch, pull up B in last lp, ch 3 with B (counts as dc), turn.

Rep rows 2 and 3 for pattern, alternating colors A, B, and C, for 54" (137 cm) from beg. Fasten off all yarns.

FINISHING
1. Weave in ends using tapestry needle.
2. To create fringe, wind all three colors of yarn several times around an 8" (20 cm) piece of cardboard, cut one end. Rep until 60 16" (40 cm) strands have been cut—20 strands of each color. Holding one strand of each color together for each fringe, fold strands in half, insert a crochet hook from back to front through the right-hand corner of one scarf end, and pull the folded end of the strands through the scarf. Bring strand ends through the loop and pull firmly to knot. Rep across for a total of 10 knots on each end of scarf. Trim fringe even if necessary.

Fun Fur Stripes Scarf

Feel like a diva in this funky fur scarf hooked in

alternating stripes of fur and wool-blend yarn. Look

closely at the wool stripes, and you'll see rows of tiny

bobbles, an extra detail.

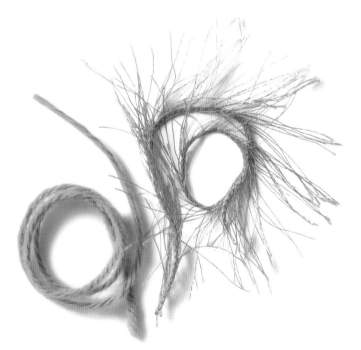

YARN

Medium-weight acrylic/wool blend yarn

Shown: Wool-Ease by Lion Brand Yarn, 80% acrylic/20% wool, 3 oz (85 g)/197 yd (180 m): Turquoise #148, 1 skein (A)

Bulky-weight novelty fur yarn

Shown: Fun Fur by Lion Brand Yarn, 100% polyester, 1.75 oz (50 g)/64 yd (50 m): Turquoise #148, 3 skeins (B)

HOOK

Size $10\frac{1}{2}$/K (6.5 mm)

STITCH USED

Single crochet

GAUGE

$10\frac{1}{2}$ sts = 4" (10 cm) on $10\frac{1}{2}$/K hook

NOTION

Tapestry needle

FINISHED SIZE

5" (13 cm) wide and 68" (172 cm) long

47

Alternating stripes of fur yarn and smooth yarn give the scarf a posh faux fur look.

SCARF

When changing colors, do not fasten off yarn after each stripe, but carry it up sides.

Foundation row: With A, ch 18. Starting in second ch from hook, work 1 sc in each ch (17 sc), ch 1 (counts as sc now and throughout), turn.

Row 1: Sl st in first st (do not sk 1), pick up lp in next st and in that lp ch 3, yo, and pull through both lps on hook (bobble made), * 1 sc in next st, pick up lp in next st and in that lp ch 3, yo, and through both lps on hook, rep from * across, 1 sc in last st (8 bobbles), ch 1, turn.

Row 2: Sk first st, 1 sc in each of next 15 sts, 1 sc in top of tch, pull up B in last lp, ch 1 with B, turn.

Three-chain bobbles give the smooth-yarn stripes a pebbly look (shown without the fur for clarity).

Row 3: With B, rep row 2, turn.

Row 4: Rep row 3, pull up A in last lp, ch 1 with A, turn.

Rep rows 1–4 for 68" (172 cm), end row 2.

FINISHING
Weave in ends using tapestry needle.

Peaches and Cream Scarf

This summery peaches-and-cream scarf gets its

airy texture from a lofty yarn and a shell-stitch

pattern.

YARN

Lightweight cotton/rayon
blend yarn

Shown: Milano by Newton
Country, 65% cotton/35%
rayon, 4 oz (113 g)/220 yd
(202 m): Peach/White Tweed,
1 skein

HOOK

Size 6/G (4.5 mm)

STITCHES USED

Single crochet

Double crochet

Triple crochet

Triple crochet 3 together

GAUGE

1 tr3tog cluster = 2" (10 cm)
on 6/G hook

NOTION

Tapestry needle

FINISHED SIZE

5" (13 cm) wide and 48"
(122 cm) long

Leaf-shaped clusters are worked in both directions from a center foundation row.

SCARF

First half of scarf is worked first, then second half is picked up from beg of first half and worked out to the end.

Foundation row: Ch 22. Starting in fifth ch from hook, work [3 dc, ch 2, 3 dc] in ch, ch 4, sk 7 ch, [1 dc, ch 4, 1 dc] in next ch, ch 4, sk 7 ch, [3 dc, ch 2, 3 dc] in next ch, sk 1 ch, 1 dc in last ch, ch 3 (counts as dc now and throughout), turn.

Row 1: Work [3 dc, ch 3, 3 dc] in next ch-2 sp, ch 2, sk 1 ch-4 sp, [1 tr3 tog, ch 3] 3 times in next ch-4 sp, 1 tr3tog in same sp, ch 2, sk 1 ch-4 sp, [3 dc, ch 2, 3 dc] in next ch-2 sp, 1 dc in top of tch, ch 3, turn.

Row 2: Work [3 dc, ch 2, 3 dc] in next ch-2 sp, ch 3, sk 1 ch-2 sp, [2 sc in next ch-3 sp, ch 3] twice, 2 sc in next ch-3 sp, ch 3, sk 1 ch-2 sp [3 dc, ch 2, 3 dc] in last ch-2 sp, 1 dc in top of tch, ch 3, turn.

Row 3: Work [3 dc, ch 2, 3 dc] in next ch-2 sp, ch 4, sk 1 ch-3 sp, 2 sc in next ch-3 sp, ch 3, 2 sc in next ch-3 sp, ch 4, sk 1 ch-3 sp, [3 dc, ch 2, 3 dc] in last ch-2 sp, 1 dc in top of tch, ch 3, turn.

Row 4: Work [3 dc, ch 2, 3 dc] in next ch-2 sp, ch 4, sk 1 ch-3 sp, [1 dc,

Strands of cotton and rayon twisted together give the yarn a two-tone tweed look.

ch 4, 1 dc] in next ch-3 sp, ch 4, sk 1 ch-3 sp, [3 dc, ch 2, 3 dc] in next ch-2 sp, 1 dc in top of tch, ch 3, turn.

Rep rows 1–4 for 24" (61 cm) from beg, fasten off.

SECOND HALF OF SCARF

Join yarn in right corner of beg of scarf, ch 3.

Foundation row: Work [3 dc, ch 2, 3 dc] in same ch as dc cluster, ch 4, sk 7 ch, [1 dc, ch 4, 1 dc] in same ch as dcs, ch 4, sk 7 ch, [3 dc, ch 2, 3 dc] in same ch as dc cluster, sk 1 ch, 1 dc in same ch as dc.

Rep rows 1–4 for 24" (61 cm) from beg, fasten off.

FINISHING

Weave in ends using tapestry needle.

Mixed Greens Scarf

Four unusual yarns combine for drama and flair.

Soft and sumptuous with a wonderful blend of

color and texture, this simple scarf is a pleasure

to crochet.

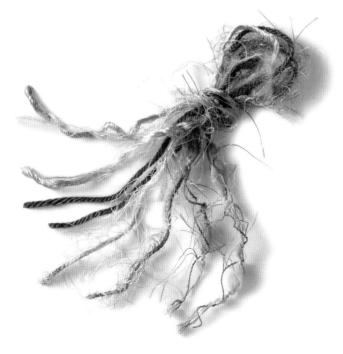

YARN

Bulky-weight rayon/mohair
blend yarn

Shown: Kid Slique by Prism,
66% rayon/26% kid mohair/
8% nylon, 2 oz (57 g)/88 yd
(81 m): Arroyo, 1 skein (A)

Bulky-weight eyelash
novelty yarn

Shown: Linie 43 Punta by On-
Line, 45% rayon/45% nylon/
10% acrylic, 1.75 oz (50 g)/88
yd (81 m): #15, 1 skein (B)

Bulky-weight novelty yarn

Shown: Bugia by Trendsetter,
70% Tactel/30% polyester,
1.75 oz (50 g)/85 yd (80 m):
#15, 1 skein (C)

Bulky-weight eyelash yarn

Shown: Coconut by Trendsetter,
100% polyester, 1.75 oz (50 g)/
66 yd (61 m): #118, 1 skein (D)

HOOK

Size 10½/K (6.5 mm)

STITCHES USED

Single crochet

Half double crochet

Double crochet

GAUGE

7 dc = 4" (10 cm) on
10½/K hook

NOTION

Tapestry needle

FINISHED SIZE

6" (15 cm) wide and 64"
(162 cm) long

Scarf is worked side to side in stripes of four yarns, each with distinctive colors and textures.

SCARF

All rows are worked tbl.

Foundation row: With A, ch 120 loosely. Starting in third ch from hook, work 1 dc in each ch across row (117 dc), ch 1, turn.

Row 1: Sk first st, * work 1 sc in next st, rep from * across, 1 sc in top of tch, ch 3 (counts as dc now and throughout), turn.

Row 2: Sk first st, * work 1 dc in next st, rep from * across, 1 dc in top of tch, pull up B in last lp, ch 3 with B, turn,

Row 3: With B, rep row 2.

Row 4: Sk first st, * work 1 hdc in next st, rep from * across, 1 hdc in top of tch, pull up C in last lp, ch 3 with C, turn.

Row 5: With C, rep row 2.

Row 6: Rep row 4, pull up D in last lp, ch 3 with D, turn.

Row 7: With D, rep row 2.

Row 8: Rep row 4.

Row 9: Rep row 2.

Row 10: Rep row 4, fasten off.

FINISHING

Weave in ends using tapestry needle.

Loopy Ridges Scarf

Rows of loops give this scarf a trendy ruffled look, and the luxurious alpaca-blend yarn has classic appeal. The scarf is incredibly soft and warm.

YARN

Medium-weight alpaca/wool yarn

Shown: Suri Merino by Plymouth Yarn Company, 55% Suri alpaca/45% extra-fine merino wool, 1.75 oz (50 g)/109 yd (100 m): #2037, 3 balls

HOOK

Size 8/H (5 mm)

STITCHES USED

Single crochet
Double crochet

GAUGE

15 dc = 4" (10 cm) on 8/H hook

NOTION

Tapestry needle

FINISHED SIZE

5" (13 cm) wide and 48" (122 cm) long

Alpaca/wool yarn in alternating rows of double crochet and chain-stitch loops.

SCARF

Foundation row: Ch 23. Starting in fifth ch from hook, work 1 dc in each ch (19 dc), ch 1, turn.

Row 1: (WS) Work 1 sc in first st, * ch 7, 1 sc tbl in each of next 2 sc, rep from * 8 times more, ch 7, 1 sc in top of tch, ch1, turn (10 loops).

Row 2: Work Sl st in first st, ch 3 (counts as dc now and throughout), dc tbl in each of the next 18 sts, 1 dc in top of tch (20 dc), ch 3, turn.

Working stitches through the back loop keeps the loopy ridges on the front of the scarf.

Rows 3–4: Sk first dc, working in both loops, work 1 dc in each of the next 18 dc, 1 dc in top of tch, ch 1, turn.

Rep rows 1–4 for 48" (122 cm), end row 2, fasten off.

FINISHING
Weave in ends using tapestry needle.

Cuddly Pompoms Scarf

If you're looking for instant gratification, you'll find it in this cuddly

scarf. It's nothing more than four rows of double crochet, but the

chenille yarn adds richness and depth, and

the pompom trim is a fun detail.

Chenille yarn worked in double crochet with a large hook.

YARN
Bulky-weight chenille yarn

Shown: Chenille Thick & Quick
by Lion Brand Yarn, 91%
acrylic/9% rayon, weight
varies/100 yd (92 m):
Grass Green #130, 1 skein

HOOK
11/L (8 mm)

STITCH USED
Double crochet

GAUGE
4½ dc = 4" (10 cm) on size
11/L hook

NOTIONS
Tapestry needle
3" (7.5 cm) piece of cardboard

FINISHED SIZE
5" (13 cm) wide and 68"
(173 cm) long

SCARF
Scarf is worked lengthwise.

Foundation row: Ch 85 loosely. Starting in fourth ch from hook, work 1 dc in each ch across (83 dc), ch 3 (counts as dc now and throughout), turn.

Row 1: Sk first st, * 1 dc in next st, rep from * across, 1 dc in top of tch, ch 3, turn.

Rep row 1 twice more, fasten off.

POMPOMS
Make two.

Cut two 18" (46 cm) pieces of yarn for tying pompoms; set aside. Cut 3" (7.5 cm) square of firm cardboard. Wrap yarn 30 times around cardboard. Carefully remove wraps from cardboard and tie securely in center, leave long ends of ties for sewing to scarf. Cut lps, shake out, and trim to form ball.

FINISHING
1. Weave in ends using tapestry needle.
2. Thread a length of yarn on tapestry needle and gather up ends of scarf.
3. Using long ends of pompom ties, sew pompoms to gathered ends of scarf.

Blooming Ascot

Step into spring with this soft, feminine ascot.

A slit at one end of the scarf allows you to pull

the other end through for an adjustable fit, and

a flower adds a decorative touch.

YARN

Medium-weight cotton/nylon blend yarn

Shown: Fay by Lang Yarns, 90% cotton/10% nylon, 1.75 oz (50 g)/97 yd (90 m): #0059, 2 skeins

HOOK

Size 8/H (5 mm)

STITCHES USED

Single crochet

Double crochet

GAUGE

12½ dc = 4" (10 cm) on 8/H hook

NOTION

Tapestry needle

FINISHED SIZE

7" (18 cm) wide and 44" (112 cm) long

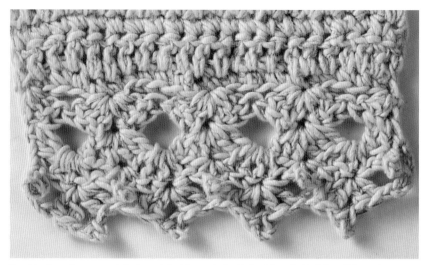

Scarf is alternating rows of single and double crochet with feminine picot edging at the ends.

SCARF

Foundation row: Ch 22. Starting in second ch from hook, work 1 sc in each ch across (21 sc), ch 3 (counts as dc now and throughout), turn.

Row 1: Sk first st, work 1 dc in each of next 19 sts, 1 dc in tch (21 dc), ch 1 (counts as sc now and throughout), turn.

Row 2: Sk first st, work 1 sc in each of next 19 sts, 1 sc in top of tch (21 sc), ch 3, turn.

Rep rows 1 and 2 for 33" (84 cm) from beg.

Form opening as foll:

Next row: Beg with row 1, work 1 dc in each of next 9 sts, ch 1, turn. Cont to rep rows 1 and 2 over these 10 sts for 2" (5 cm), end row 2, fasten off.

Sk 1 st at center of scarf at opening edge, rejoin yarn, ch 3. Beg with row 1, work 1 dc in each of 9 rem sts. Cont to rep rows 1 and 2 over these 10 sts for 2" (5 cm), end at outside edge and with row 2. Ch 3, turn, work 10 dc (first opening half), ch 1, 10 dc across rem sts (second opening half).

Rep rows 1 and 2 across all 21 sts for 40" (102 cm) from beg, end row 2. Ch 3, turn, work edging as foll:

EDGING

Row 1: Work 2 dc in same st as tch, * sk 4 st, [3 dc, ch 2, 3 dc] in next st (shell made); rep from * across, sk 4 sc, 3 dc in top of tch, ch 2, turn.

Crocheted flower is sewn onto the scarf next to the opening.

Row 2: Work 2 dc in same st as tch, * ch 1, [3 dc, ch 2, 3 dc] in ch-2 sp of next shell; rep from * across, ch 1, 3 dc in top of tch, ch 4, turn.

Row 3: Work 1 Sl st in fourth ch from hook, 1 sc in same st as tch, * 3 dc in ch-1 sp, [1 sc, ch 4, Sl st in fourth ch from hook, 1 sc] in ch-2 sp of next shell (picot group made). Rep from * once, 3 dc in ch-1 sp, 1 sc in top of tch, ch 4, Sl st in fourth ch from hook, Sl st in last sc worked, ch 5, turn.

Row 4: * Work [2 dc, ch 4, Sl st in fourth ch from hook, 2 dc] in center dc of 3-dc group, rep from * across, ch 5, sl st in last st, fasten off.

Work other end of scarf to correspond.

FLOWER
Foundation rnd: Ch 1 (center), ch 3 (counts as dc), work 11 dc in beg ch, join with Sl st to top of beg ch 3 (12 dc).

Rnd 1: Ch 1, work [1 sc, ch 1, 1 sc] in same st as ch 1, * ch 1, [1 sc, ch 1, 1 sc] in FL of next st; rep from * around, ch 1, join with Sl st in both loops of first sc (center petals made).

Rnd 2: Holding center petals forward and working in BL of foundation rnd, [1 sc, ch 2, 1 dc, 1 tr, ch 3, Sl st in first ch of ch-3, 1 tr, 1 dc, ch 2] in each st around, fasten off.

FINISHING
1. With the opening end of the scarf pointing toward you, position flower on the left side of the opening, centering it on the opening. Using tapestry needle and the loose end from beg of flower, sew flower securely onto scarf.
2. Weave in ends using tapestry needle.

Funky
Curves Scarf

Perfect for a last-minute holiday gift, this funky,

cozy scarf, made with a super-bulky yarn, is

completed in only six rows.

YARN

Super-bulky-weight wool yarn
in two colors

Shown: Baby by Tahki,
100% merino wool, 3.5 oz
(100 g)/60 yd (55 m):
#62 (green), 2 skeins (A);
#60 (rose), 1 skein (B)

HOOK

Size 15/P (11.5 mm)

STITCHES USED

Single crochet

Half double crochet

Double crochet

Triple crochet

GAUGE

6 dc = 4" (10 cm) on
15/P hook

NOTIONS

Tapestry needle

8" (20 cm) piece of cardboard

FINISHED SIZE

5" (13 cm) wide and 68"
(172 cm) long

Stitches progress from single to half double to double to triple crochet and back again.

SCARF

Scarf is worked lengthwise.

Foundation row: With A, ch 99. Starting in second ch from hook, work 1 sc in each ch across (98 sc), ch 1 (counts as sc now and throughout), turn.

Row 1: Sk first st, work 1 sc in each sc, 1 sc in tch, pull up B in last lp, ch 3 with B (counts as tr now and throughout), turn.

Row 2: With B, sk first st, work 1 tr in next st, 1 dc in each of next 2 sts, 1 hdc in next st, 1 sc in next st, * ch 2, sk 2 sts, 1 sc in next st, 1 hdc in next st, 1 dc in each of next 2 sts, 1 tr in each of next 2 sts, 1 dc in each of next 2 sts, 1 hdc in next st, 1 sc in next st, rep from * to last 8 sts, ch 2, sk 2 sts, 1 sc in next st, 1 hdc in next st, 1 dc in each of next 2 sts, 1 tr in next st, 1 tr in top of tch, ch 3, turn.

Row 3: Sk first tr, work 1 tr in next tr, 1 dc in each of next 2 dc, 1 hdc in next hdc, 1 sc in next sc, * ch 2, sk 2, 1 sc in next sc, 1 hdc in next hdc, 1 dc in each of next 2 dc, 1 tr in each of next 2 tr, 1 dc in each of next 2 dc, 1 hdc in next hdc, 1 sc in next sc, rep from * to last 8 sts, ch 2, sk 2, 1 sc in next sc, 1 hdc in next hdc, 1 dc in each of next 2 dc, 1 tr in next tr, 1 trc in top of tch, pull up A in last lp, ch 1 with A, turn.

Fringe is made with strands of both yarn colors.

Row 4: With A, sk 1, work 1 sc in each of next 5 sts, [1 sc into each of the 2 unworked sc in row 1 (last A row), working over and enclosing ch-2 from previous rows],* 1 sc in each of next 10 sc, rep [ ], rep from * to last 6 sts, 1 sc in each of next 5 sts, 1 sc in top of tch, ch 1, turn.

Row 5: Sk first st, work 1 sc in each st across, 1 sc in top of tch, fasten off.

FINISHING

1. Weave in ends using tapestry needle.

2. To create fringe, wind both colors of yarn several times around an 8" (20 cm) piece of cardboard, cut one end. Rep until 32 16" (40 cm) strands have been cut—16 strands of each color. Holding one strand of each color together for each fringe, fold strands in half, insert a crochet hook from back to front through the right-hand corner of one scarf end, and pull the folded end of the strands through the scarf. Bring strand ends through the loop and pull firmly to knot. Rep across for a total of 8 knots on each end of scarf. Trim fringe even if necessary.

Handsome Basket-Weave Scarf

A textured stitch pattern, worked in a regal cashmere

and silk yarn, creates a warm and elegant scarf. The basket-

weave stitch only looks complicated. Once you've mastered the

pattern repeat, hooking it is a snap.

Alternate groups of back post and front post double crochet stitches mimic a basket weave.

SCARF

Foundation row: Ch 33. Starting in fifth ch from hook, work 1 dc in each ch across (30 dc), ch 3 (counts as 1 dc now and throughout), turn.

Rows 1, 3, 6, and 8: Sk first st, * work 4 FPdc, 4 BPdc, rep from * across, 4 FPdc, 1 dc in top of tch, ch 3, turn.

Rows 2, 4, 5, and 7: Sk first st, * work 4 BPdc, 4 FPdc, rep from * across, 4 BPdc, 1 dc in top of tch, ch 3, turn.

Rep rows 1–8 for 48" (122 cm) from beg. Fasten off.

FINISHING

1. Weave in ends using tapestry needle.
2. To create fringe, wind yarn several times around a 4" (10 cm) piece of cardboard, cut one end. Rep until 80 8" (20 cm) strands have been cut. Holding 2 strands together for each fringe, fold strands in half, insert a crochet hook from back to front through the right-hand corner of one scarf end, and pull the folded end of the strands through the scarf. Bring strand ends through the loop and pull firmly to knot. Rep across for a total of 20 knots on each end of scarf. Trim fringe even if necessary.

YARN

Medium-weight cashmere/silk yarn

Shown: Kashmir by Trendsetter, 65% cashmere/35% silk, 1.75 oz (50 g)/110 yd (100 m): #9, 7 balls

HOOK

Size 8/H (5 mm)

STITCHES USED

Double crochet

Front post double crochet

Back post double crochet

GAUGE

16 dc = 4" (10 cm) on 8/H hook

NOTIONS

Tapestry needle

4" (10 cm) piece of cardboard

FINISHED SIZE

7½" (19 cm) wide and 48" (122 cm) long

Cotton
Candy Scarf

This fluffy confection has only five rows.

Worked with a super-bulky yarn, it's as

quick to crochet as it is fun to wear.

Super-bulky, super-soft yarn is crocheted on a large hook.

YARN
Super-bulky-weight
acrylic/nylon blend bouclé yarn

Shown: Bliss by Caron, 60%
acrylic/40% nylon, 1.75 oz
(50 g)/82 yd (75 m): Cotton
Candy #0002, 3 skeins

HOOK
Size 11/L (8 mm)

STITCH USED
Double crochet

GAUGE
7 dc = 4" (10 cm) on
11/L hook

NOTIONS
Tapestry needle
8" (20 cm) piece of cardboard

FINISHED SIZE
4" (10 cm) wide and 58"
(147 cm) long

SCARF

Scarf is worked lengthwise.

Foundation row: Ch 108 loosely. Starting in fifth ch from hook, work 1 dc in each ch across (104 dc), ch 5, turn.

Row 1: Sk first st, 1 dc in next st, * ch 1, sk 1, 1 dc in next st, rep from *, ch 1, sk 1, 1 dc in top of tch, ch 3, turn.

Row 2: * Work 2 dc in ch-1 sp, rep from * across, 1 dc in third ch of tch, ch 5, turn.

Rep rows 1 and 2 once more, fasten off.

FINISHING

1. Weave in ends using tapestry needle.
2. To create fringe, wind yarn several times around an 8" (20 cm) piece of cardboard, cut one end. Rep until 32 16" (40 cm) strands have been cut. Holding 2 strands together for each fringe, fold strands in half, insert a crochet hook from back to front through the right-hand corner of one scarf end, and pull the folded end of the strands through the scarf. Bring strand ends through the loop and pull firmly to knot. Rep across for a total of 8 knots on each end of scarf. Trim fringe even if necessary.

Totally Twisted Scarf

The twist in this scarf only looks complicated. Two strips are worked separately in single crochet and contrasting colors, then twisted together at the end. A bulky yarn and short rows make it work up quickly.

YARN

Bulky-weight wool yarn in two colors

Shown: Lopi by Reynolds, 100% Icelandic wool, 3.5oz (100 g)/110 yd (101 m): #2, 1 skein (A); #209, 1 skein (B)

HOOK

Size 10½/K (6.5 mm)

STITCH USED

Single crochet

GAUGE

10 sc = 4" (10 cm) on 10½/K hook

NOTIONS

Tapestry needle

7" (18 cm) piece of cardboard

FINISHED SIZE

5" (13 cm) wide and 58" (147 cm) long

Bulky wool yarn in single crochet is worked up in two narrow strips of coordinating colors.

SCARF

Make two strips, one in each color.

Foundation row: Ch 7. Starting in second ch from hook, work 1 sc in each ch across (6 sc), ch 1 (counts as sc), turn.

Row 1: Sk the first st, work 1 sc in each of next 4 sc, 1 sc in tch (6 sc).

Rep row 1 for 58" (147 cm), fasten off.

FINISHING

1. When both strips are finished, lay them side by side, pin one end tog, and twist them over and under each other loosely, keeping strips flat and pinning as you go. With a tapestry needle and a length of yarn, sew the strips together.

2. Weave in ends using tapestry needle.

3. To create fringe, wind both colors of yarn several times around a 7" (18 cm) piece of cardboard, cut one end. Rep until 40 14" (35.5 cm) strands have been cut—20 strands of each color. Holding one strand of each color together for each fringe, fold strands in half, insert a crochet hook from back to front through the right-hand corner of one scarf end, and pull the folded end of the strands through the scarf. Bring strand ends through the loop and pull firmly to knot. Rep across for a total of 10 knots on each end of scarf. Trim fringe even if necessary.

Strips are crisscrossed and hand-stitched together.

Crochet Stitches

SLIP KNOT AND CHAIN

All crochet begins with a chain, into which is worked the foundation row for your piece. To make a chain, start with a slip knot. To make a slip knot, make a loop several inches from the end of the yarn, insert the hook through the loop, and catch the tail with the end **(1)**. Draw the yarn through the loop on the hook **(2)**. After the slip knot, start your chain. Wrap the yarn over the hook (yarn over) and catch it with the hook. Draw the yarn through the loop on the hook. You have now made 1 chain. Repeat the process to make a row of chains. When counting chains, do not count the slip knot at the beginning or the loop that is on the hook **(3)**.

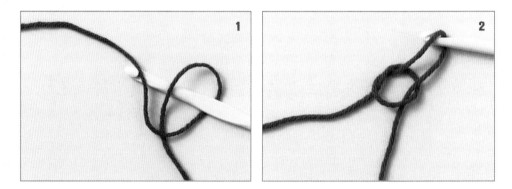

SLIP STITCH

The slip stitch is a very short stitch, which is mainly used to join 2 pieces of crochet together when working in rounds. To make a slip stitch, insert the hook into the specified stitch, wrap the yarn over the hook **(1)**, and then draw the yarn through the stitch and the loop already on the hook **(2)**.

SINGLE CROCHET

Insert the hook into the specified stitch, wrap the yarn over the hook, and draw the yarn through the stitch so there are 2 loops on the hook **(1)**. Wrap the yarn over the hook again and draw the yarn through both loops **(2)**. When working in single crochet, always insert the hook through both top loops of the next stitch, unless the directions specify front loop or back loop only.

SINGLE CROCHET TWO STITCHES TOGETHER

This decreases the number of stitches in a row or round by 1. Insert the hook into the specified stitch, wrap the yarn over the hook, and draw the yarn through the stitch so there are 2 loops on the hook. Insert the hook through the next stitch, wrap the yarn over the hook, and draw the yarn through the stitch so there are 3 loops on the hook **(1).** Wrap the yarn over the hook again and draw the yarn through all the loops at once **(2).**

SINGLE CROCHET THREE STITCHES TOGETHER

This decreases the number of stitches in a row or round by 2. Follow the directions for single crochet two stitches together, but draw up a loop in the third stitch so there are 4 loops on the hook before wrapping the yarn and drawing through all the loops at once.

SINGLE CROCHET THROUGH THE BACK LOOP

This creates a distinct ridge on the side facing you. Insert the hook through the back loop only of each stitch, rather than under both loops of the stitch. Complete the single crochet as usual.

REVERSE SINGLE CROCHET

This stitch is usually used to create a border. At the end of a row, chain 1 but do not turn. Working backward, insert the hook into the previous stitch **(1),** wrap the yarn over the hook, and draw the yarn through the stitch so there are 2 loops on the hook. Wrap the yarn over the hook again and draw the yarn through both loops. Continue working in the reverse direction **(2).**

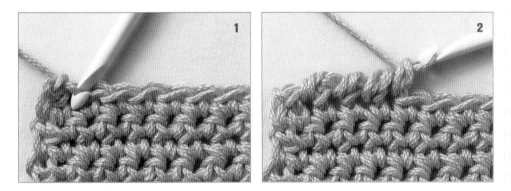

HALF DOUBLE CROCHET

Wrap the yarn over the hook, insert the hook into the specified stitch, and wrap the yarn over the hook again. Draw the yarn through the stitch so there are 3 loops on the hook **(1)**. Wrap the yarn over the hook and draw it through all 3 loops at once **(2)**.

DOUBLE CROCHET

Wrap the yarn over the hook, insert the hook into the specified stitch, and wrap the yarn over the hook again. Draw the yarn through the stitch so there are 3 loops on the hook **(1).** Wrap the yarn over the hook again and draw it through 2 of the loops so there are now 2 loops on the hook **(2).** Wrap the yarn over the hook again and draw it through the last 2 loops **(3).**

DOUBLE CROCHET TWO STITCHES TOGETHER

This decreases the number of stitches in a row or round by 1. Wrap the yarn over the hook, insert the hook into the specified stitch, and wrap the yarn over the hook again. Draw the yarn through the stitch so there are 3 loops on the hook. Wrap the yarn over the hook again and draw it through 2 of the loops so there are now 2 loops on the hook. Wrap the yarn over the hook and pick up a loop in the next stitch, so there are now 4 loops on the hook. Wrap the yarn over the hook and draw through 2 loops, yarn over and draw through 3 loops to complete the stitch.

TRIPLE, OR TREBLE, CROCHET

Wrap the yarn over the hook twice, insert the hook into the specified stitch, and wrap the yarn over the hook again. Draw the yarn through the stitch so there are 4 loops on the hook. Wrap the yarn over the hook again **(1)** and draw it through 2 of the loops so there are now 3 loops on the hook **(2).** Wrap the yarn over the hook again and draw it through 2 of the loops so there are now 2 loops on the hook **(3).** Wrap the yarn over the hook again and draw it through the last 2 loops **(4).**

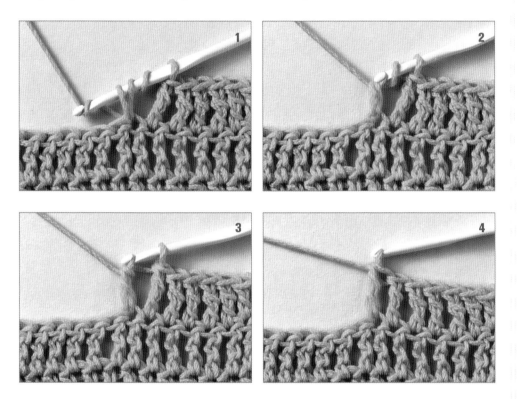

TRIPLE CROCHET TWO STITCHES TOGETHER

This decreases the number of stitches in a row or round by 1. Follow the directions for triple crochet until you have two loops left on the hook. Wrap the yarn over the hook twice, pick up a loop in the next stitch, so there are now 5 loops on the hook. * Wrap the yarn over the hook and draw through 2 loops. Repeat from * until there are 3 loops left on the hook. Wrap the yarn over and pull through all 3 loops to complete the stitch.

DOUBLE TRIPLE CROCHET

Wrap the yarn over the hook 3 times, insert the hook into the specified stitch, and wrap the yarn over the hook again. Draw the yarn through the stitch so there are 5 loops on the hook. Wrap the yarn over the hook again and draw it through 2 of the loops so there are now 4 loops on the hook. Wrap the yarn over the hook again and draw it through 2 of the loops so there are now 3 loops on the hook. Wrap the yarn over the hook again and draw it through 2 of the loops so there are now 2 loops on the hook. Wrap the yarn over the hook again and draw it through the last 2 loops.

FRONT POST DOUBLE CROCHET

This stitch follows a row of double crochet.

Chain 3 to turn. Wrap the yarn over the hook. Working from the front, insert the hook from right to left (left to right for left-handed crocheters) under the post of the first double crochet from the previous row, and pick up a loop (shown). Wrap the yarn over the hook and complete the stitch as a double crochet.

Left-handed.

Right-handed.

BACK POST DOUBLE CROCHET

This stitch follows a row of double crochet. Chain 3 to turn. Wrap the yarn over the hook. Working from the back, insert the hook from right to left (left to right for left-handed crocheters) under the post of the first double crochet from the previous row, and pick up a loop (shown). Wrap the yarn over the hook and complete the stitch as a double crochet.

Left-handed.

Right-handed.

FRONT POST TRIPLE CROCHET

Wrap the yarn over the hook twice. Working from the front, insert the hook from right to left (left to right for left-handed crocheters) under the post of the indicated stitch in the row below, and pick up a loop (shown). Wrap the yarn over the hook and complete the triple crochet stitch as usual.

Left-handed.

Right-handed.

SHELL STITCH

Make 2 double crochets, chain 1, and then work 2 more double crochets in the same stitch (shown). This is often called a cluster. In the following row, work the same cluster into the space created by the chain stitch.

BOBBLE STITCH

Wrap the yarn over the hook and pick up a loop in the next stitch. Wrap the yarn over the hook again and pull it through 2 of the stitches on the hook. Repeat this 5 times in the same stitch. Then wrap the yarn over the hook and pull it through all 6 loops on the hook. The bobble stitch is worked from the wrong side and pushed to right side of the work.

PUFF STITCH

This stitch is worked the same as the Bobble Stitch (opposite), but not necessarily from the wrong side. Because it is preceded and followed by double crochet stitches, this Puff Stitch is flatter than the Bobble Stitch.

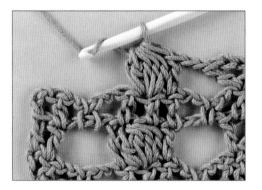

LOOSE PUFF STITCH

This stitch is worked the same as the Puff Stitch (above) and Bobble Stitch (opposite), but the loops are pulled up to at least $\frac{1}{2}$" (1.3 cm) long.

INTERLOCKING BLOCK STITCH

Each yarn is worked across one row and then left hanging at the side while each of two other yarns are worked in the following two rows. Yarns are carried loosely up the sides by twisting them once together with the working yarn.

Foundation row: With color A, chain 23.

Row 1: Continuing with color A, skip the first 3 chains (this counts as a double crochet), then work 1 double crochet in each of the next 2 chains. * Chain 3, skip 3, work 1 double crochet in each of the next 3 chains **(1).** Repeat from * across the row, pull up color B in the last loop (drop color A), and turn.

Row 2: With B, * chain 3, skip the next 3 stitches, work 1 double crochet in each of the next 3 chains that were skipped in row 1, working over and enclosing the 3 chains hooked in the previous row **(2).** Repeat from * across the row, ending chain 3, skip 2 stitches, single crochet in the top of the turning chain, pull up color C in last loop (drop B), and turn.

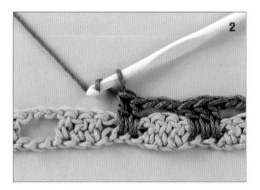

Row 3: With C, chain 3 (this counts as a double crochet), then work 1 double cro- chet in each of the next 2 stitches from two rows below (color A), working over the 3 chain stitches from the previous row (color B) **(3).** * Chain 3, skip 3, work 1 dou- ble crochet in each of the next 3 stitches from two rows below, working over the 3 chain stitches from the previous row. Repeat from * across the row, pull up color A in last loop, and turn.

Row 4: With A, repeat row 2, working the double crochets in the stitches two rows below, working over the chain stitches from the previous row.

Repeat rows 3 and 4 for the pattern, changing colors every row.

Abbreviations

approx	approximately	**oz**	ounce(s)
beg	begin/beginning	**p**	picot
bet	between	**patt**	pattern
BL	back loop(s)	**pc**	popcorn
BP	back post	**pm**	place marker
BPdc	back post double crochet	**prev**	previous
CC	contrasting color	**rem**	remain/remaining
ch	chain	**rep**	repeat(s)
ch-	refers to chain or space previously made, e.g., ch-1 space	**rev sc**	reverse single crochet
		rnd(s)	round(s)
ch lp	chain loop	**RS**	right side(s)
ch-sp	chain space	**sc**	single crochet
CL	cluster(s)	**sc3tog**	single crochet 3 stitches together
cm	centimeter(s)		
cont	continue	**sk**	skip
dc	double crochet	**Sl st**	slip stitch
dc2tog	double crochet 2 stitches together	**sp(s)**	space(s)
		st(s)	stitch(es)
dec	decrease/decreases/ decreasing	**tch**	turning chain
		tbl	through back loop(s)
dtr	double triple crochet	**tog**	together
FL	front loop(s)	**tr**	triple crochet
foll	follow/follows/following	**tr2tog**	triple crochet 2 together
FP	front post	**WS**	wrong side(s)
FPdc	front post double crochet	**yd**	yard(s)
FPtr	front post triple crochet	**yo**	yarn over
g	gram(s)	**yoh**	yarn over hook
hdc	half double crochet	**[ ]**	Work instructions within brackets as many times as directed
inc	increase/increases/ increasing	**( )**	At end of row, indicates total number of stitches worked
lp(s)	loop(s)	*****	Repeat instructions following the single asterisk as directed
m	meter(s)		
MC	main color	******	Repeat instructions between asterisks as many times as directed or repeat from a given set of instructions
mm	millimeter(s)		